Micheál Ó Conghaile is an award-winning writer and publisher from Connemara, Co. Galway. He established the publishing company Cló Iar-Chonnacht (CIC) in 1985. He has written many books in Irish, mostly short story collections. He won the Hennessy Literary Award in 1997, and he was also awarded the Hennessy Young Irish Writer of the Year Award. In 1998 he was elected to Aosdána. His works have been translated into various languages, including Romanian, Croatian, Albanian, Slovenian, German, Bengali, Polish, Macedonian and Arabic, and three of his books are available in English: *The Connemara Five* (Arlen Press), *The Colours of Man* (CIC) and *Rambling Jack* (Dalkey Archive Press). He was writer in residence at Queen's University Belfast and at the University of Ulster, Coleraine, from 1999 to 2002.

Colourful Irish Phrases

Micheál Ó Conghaile

MERCIER PRESS
IRISH PUBLISHER - IRISH STORY

MERCIER PRESS

Cork

www.mercierpress.ie

© Micheál Ó Conghaile, 2018

Published in association with  Cló Iar-Chonnacht

ISBN: 978 1 78117 555 2

10 9 8 7 6 5 4 3 2 1

A CIP record for this title is available from the British
Library

Printed and bound in the EU.

Contents

Introduction

I remember not being able to speak English. Growing up in the 1960s on a small island, Inis Treabhair, off the Connemara coast, Irish was the everyday language of its dwindling population of about forty people. Six households in all. The reason I remember so clearly not being able to speak English is the summer visits when our first cousins from London and Galway city would come to spend a few weeks with us. I must have been three or four years old at the time. As kids, they spoke only English. I spoke only Irish. But we got along and played together, communicating with each other as children from different backgrounds do. I picked up some English from them and later learned English at school, where every subject except English was taught through Irish. When I entered the island's national school in 1966 there were twenty-one students enrolled there; when I left in 1975 the number had dwindled to five. The school doors were locked for the last time in 1980, the numbers having fallen to two.

The same fate awaited life on the island. In the 1870s when its population peaked, 171 people lived there. A couple of years ago the last native islander, Patsy Lydon, left the island to live with family members on the mainland, bringing an end to island life which had gone on unbroken for at least 200 years.

So much dies with the death of island life. Even in the future, if other people go to live there, the chain or the link to the original inhabitants will be forever broken. It was the islanders and their forefathers who named and knew every field and hillock on the island; its strands, inlets, shores and rocks; the surrounding tides and currents and waves they had to navigate in all sorts of weather; the joys and pains of hundreds of years of continued life; the local lore, songs, poems

8

and stories. And the language – the language that brought everything to life. In this case it was Irish.

The Irish language phrases in this book are ones that I mostly grew up with. Others I picked up over the years. Most of them were part of what we were, of our daily speech and lives. Perhaps some of them originated on the island. Most of them can be heard from native Irish speakers from all Gaeltachtaí in Ireland, still very much alive and in use. We don't know for sure how old they are. Some of them may have been used for over 1,000 years, originating in Old Irish before the ninth century, living through Middle Irish, 900–1200, through Classical Irish, 1200–1600, and still to the fore in Modern Irish, surviving through the Great Famine of the 1840s and the decline of the language in most parts of the country. We know for sure that one of them, the phrase *Fáilte Uí Cheallaigh*, the O'Kelly welcome, is nearly 700 years old and it's still very much in use.

I am grateful to John Spillane at Mercier Press for asking me to put this collection of phrases together. Growing up with these phrases, I had taken them for granted and did not think much of them. After all, most of the time we use language just to communicate. That's all. Until I did a little research, I was not aware that most of these phrases were not familiar to English speakers in Ireland. Very few of them have made their way into everyday English usage. They were not translated or collected. When translated, word for word, they sound different, unusual and sometimes funny, as John pointed out to me. But above all, they are rich and deeply rooted. They have a history. They come from somewhere deep and have travelled on a long, narrow, winding path. They have meaning and often a story to tell or snatches of history to reveal, just like most of our Irish language *logainmneacha* or place names. I have included some of these stories and backgrounds in the notes. Where there is no accepted theory, I have sometimes included some speculation on my part. I'm open to be corrected in such cases and, indeed, to suggestions. As the *seanfhocal* says, '*Ní haon ualach an t-eolas*' ('Knowledge is no burden').

We are all aware of the great contribution the Irish language has made to the English language as it's spoken in Ireland and, indeed, beyond. It makes it richer and more colourful. It may seem small, but it's like the yeast in a cake making the English language rise and expand into fullness and goodness. Most of our great writers in English have taken advantage of this and it has enriched their writings and world literature in English. The likes of Joyce, Beckett and Heaney come to mind. They all dug deep and mined for golden nuggets here and there, and they delivered the goods. Of course, in Irish we have our own great writers, like Ó Cadhain, Ó Direáin and Ó Ríordáin, who immersed themselves fully in the language, its history and lore. And they faced the same odds as Joyce, Beckett and

Heaney, but with one big difference. As Ó Cadhain once said, it's difficult to write in a language that will probably be dead before you. But that did not stop him from giving it all he had, like all great writers. And he knew where he and, indeed, many other Irish language writers were coming from: *'Tá aois na Caillí Béara agam, aois Bhrú na Bóinne, aois na heilite móire. Tá dhá mhíle bliain den chráin bhréan sin arb í Éire í, ag dul timpeall i mo chluasa, i mo bhéal, i mo cheann, i mo bhrionglóidí.'* ('I'm as ancient as the Hag of Beara, as old as Newgrange, as timeless as the horn-less doe. Two thousand years of Ireland, that filthy sow, echo in my ears, in my mouth, in my head, in my dreams.')

For over 700 years now, both languages have lived side by side in this country, in people's hearts and minds. Writer and scholar Fr Peadar Ó Laoghaire (1839–1920) called it *an dá arm aigne* (the two armies of the mind). They have competed and bounced off each other over the centuries but they have also infiltrated and enriched each other. An army can fight and kill, but it can also defend and protect, and help the weak survive.

Irish writers in both languages are welcome to draw from this book. To reuse, recycle and reinvent if they feel it colours their language. After all, that's what writers do, or try to do. I would also hope that learners of the language, at whatever stage they are at, would find these phrases usable, and that a younger generation of native Irish speakers, who are not familiar with these expressions and idioms, would benefit from this word hoard. Visitors to our country who want to get some notion of our native identity will find these phrases both instructive and revealing. This small compendium of characteristic phrases will alert them to the unmistakable difference between our native language and English. Even the most basic words are expressed so differently. Please, in Irish, is *más é do thoil é* (if it is your will) and thanks becomes *go raibh maith agat* (may you receive good).

Go raibh maith agaibh to readers of this book. As the famous Irish poet and historian Seathrún Céitinn (*c.* 1580–*c.* 1644) wrote in the seventeenth century:

> *Mo bheannacht leat, a scríbhinn …/My blessing be with you, dear manuscript …*

MICHEÁL Ó CONGHAILE, 2018

Focal buíochais: A word of thanks to John Spillane and all at Mercier Press, Lochlainn Ó Tuairisg and all at Cló Iar-Chonnacht, and to the following, who read various drafts of the book and made valuable suggestions: Cathal Ó Searcaigh, Brian Ó Conchubhair, Joe Steve Ó Neachtain, Pádraic Breathnach, Pádraig Ó Siadhail, Mícheál Ó Ruairc, Lillis Ó Laoire, Alan Titley and Dónall Ó Braonáin. *Go raibh maith agaibh*.

Insults and Put-Downs

Cuir méar i do thóin.

Lit. *Put a finger in your arse.*

Feck off.

Another version I heard from an Aran Islander is
Cuir méar i do thóin is diúl í (Put a finger in your arse and
suck it).

Téigh ag feadaíl.

Lit. *Go and whistle.*

Shag off.

Tá poll i do thóin is ní fhaca tú riamh é.

Lit. *There is a hole in your arse and you never saw it.*

Normally used to finish an argument. Meaning: I don't, and will not, agree with you, so let's just move on.

Gabh agus beir i bhfad suas ort féin.

Lit. *Go and catch yourself high up.*

Feck off.

Ba dheacair é a bhearradh.

Lit. *It was hard to shave him.*

Denotes a cranky man, someone hard to please.

If an elderly man could not shave himself someone else would have to do it for him, which would not be an easy task, especially if the elderly man had a face with moles on it.

Ní bheidh muid níos suaimhní.

Lit. *We will not be any more serene or peaceful.*

Expect an argument or some aggro. Normally said (whispered) when a person who is disruptive enters the room or joins the company.

Níor mhaith liom seasamh ar chois uirthi.

Lit. *I would not like to stand on her toes.*

I wouldn't like to cross her.

Ní aithneodh sé a thochas thar a scríobadh.

Lit. *He would not know/recognise his itch from his scratch.*

He can't make his mind up. Said about a person who knows nothing. If he was itchy and scratched himself, he would not know he had scratched himself.

An béal bocht.

Lit. *The poor mouth.*

Said about a person who pretends to be a lot poorer or worse off than he is and who wants to be pitied.

This is a common phrase: *Chuir sé an béal bocht ar féin* (He put the poor mouth on himself). The words were of course made famous by the classic satirical novel *An Béal Bocht* by Myles na gCopaleen (Brian Ó Nualláin).

Ceapann sé gur as a thóin a éiríonn an ghrian.

Lit. *He thinks the sun rises from his arse.*

Ceapann sé gurb é féin a rug é féin.

Lit. *He thinks he gave birth to himself.*

Both of these would be said dismissively about a person who thinks a lot of himself.

Shílfeá gur dia beag é.

Lit. *You would think he was a small god.*

A person who thinks highly of himself and who thinks he can fix everything.

Tá cloigeann ataithe aige.

Lit. *He has a swelled head.*

He is full of himself.

Bhí sé ag dul ag déanamh cat is dhá dhrioball.

Lit. *He was going to make a cat and two tails.*

He was going to do this, that and the other. Said about a person who is all talk and no action.

Bíonn an-fháilte aige roimhe féin.

Lit. *He has a great welcome for himself.*

He thinks a lot of himself.

Codladh go headartha agus úthanna na mbó ataithe.

Lit. *Sleep until late morning and the cows' udders swell up.*

Said about a person who is lazy.

This casts an aspersion on the lazy or drunken farmer who doesn't get up in the morning and milk the cows at the proper time. The phrase is used about lazy people in general.

Ní chaitheann an chaint an t-éadach.

Lit. *Talk does not wear clothes.*

Said about a person who is all talk and no action.

Ní tharraingeodh sé na stocaí d'fhear caillte.

Lit. *He wouldn't pull the socks off a dead man.*

Said about a person who would be useless at work or who couldn't perform a simple task.

Bíodh an fheamainn aige.

Lit. *Let him have the seaweed.*

Let him go to hell.

It's difficult to explain this phrase as, in the past, seaweed was valuable and often used for manure. It might refer to the bits of seaweed that would get stuck in fishing nets, causing an obstruction, which would be a nuisance and would be thrown away. A shorter version of this phrase is *Bíodh aige* (Let him be).

Tá sé lán de chac.

Lit. *He is full of shit.*

He has a high opinion of himself.

Píobaire an aon phoirt.

Lit. The piper with the one tune.

A one-trick pony. Said about a person who is only good at one thing.

Bhí sé ag dul ina bhéal orm.

Lit. He was going in his mouth on me.

Said about a sly, sneaky person.

The phrase comes from selling cattle on a fair day. A buyer would be doing well and would have more or less agreed on a price with the seller when a third person, who would be keeping an eye on the deal from a short distance, would move in at the last minute and up the offer, leaving the first buyer empty-handed. The phrase could also be used about a man who would move in late on a courting couple and 'steal' the woman from the first man.

Ní fiú uisce na bhfataí é/
Ní fiú uisce na n-uibheacha é.

Lit. *He is not worth the potato water/
He is not worth the egg water.*

He is useless, not worth the water you would have
boiled potatoes or eggs in.

Ní fiú cac circe/an diabhail é.

Lit. *He is not worth a hen's shit/the devil's shit.*

He is useless.

Is mór an tseanmóir é.

Lit. *He is a big sermon.*

He is such a pain, hard to put up with. Mostly said
about a person who goes on and on.

Ní ar mhaithe leat é.

Lit. *It's not for your good.*

False generosity or friendship. Said about a person
who is generous or friendly for the wrong reason.
Normally they would want to get a lot more out of
the friendship than they would intend to give.

Family, Friendship and What Comes with It

Mar a chaithfeadh sé amach as a bhéal é.

Lit. *Like he threw him out of his mouth.*

He is the spitting image of his father.

Mar is dual athar/máthar dó.

Lit. *He is taking after his father/mother.*

Used to describe someone who is like a parent
in personality.

Ní ón ngealach ná ón ngrian a thóg sé é.

Lit. *It wasn't from the moon or the sun he took it.*

Ní ón ngaoth a thóg sé é.

Lit. *It wasn't from the wind he took it.*

Cá bhfágfadh sé é!

Lit. *Where would he leave it!*

Is cuid den mhuc a drioball.

Lit. *The pig's tail is part of the pig.*

All four phrases mean the same more or less. Usually said about a person who is like (takes after) his father or mother in his ways. It's nearly always used about people's bad traits, however, not their good ones! An English equivalent would be 'the apple does not fall far from the tree'.

Is cosúil le chéile an ball séire is a ghiolla.

Lit. *They are alike, the fool and his servant.*

Like father, like son.

Cuireadh fáilte Uí Cheallaigh romhainn.

Lit. *We got the O'Kelly welcome.*

We got a great welcome.

The Ó Ceallaigh mentioned is William Buí Ó
Ceallaigh, Taoiseach of Uí Mháine, who issued
an invitation to the poets, writers and artists of
Ireland to a great feast at his home, Gailey Castle
(built in 1348 on the western shores of Lough Ree,
Knockcroghery, Co. Roscommon) at Christmas
1351. The gathering was famous for William's great
hospitality and generosity. Still very common in
everyday language, even after nearly 700 years!

Rinne sé lá saoire dom.

Lit. *He made a free day (holiday) for me.*

He gave me all his time. This would normally be said if one visited a house unannounced and the host would drop everything to entertain and be with the guest.

Ag bualadh craicinn.

Lit. *Beating/hitting skin.*

Having sex.

Níor bhuail mé mo chraiceann riamh ach ar aon fhear amháin (I only ever had sex with one man) was said proudly by an older lady contrasting current norms with her own life experience.

Is breá an leath leapan í.

Lit. *She is a great half of a bed.*

She would be good to have sex with.

Tá sé in am é a chur ar an áiléar.

Lit. *It's time to put him in the loft.*

It's time for him to stop fathering children.

In the old cottages the bedroom(s) would normally be on the ground floor and there would often be a loft, used mostly for storage. Also if visitors came and if extra space was needed for sleeping, people would sleep in the loft, as would children sometimes when they got older. A ladder would be used for access to the loft before stairs became common.

It was always the man who should be sent to the loft! This phrase would never be used to refer to a woman.

Bhí lámh agus focal eatarthu.

Lit. *There was a hand and a word between them/ They had shared a word and a hand.*

They were engaged.

Bhí siad luaite i gcleamhnas.

Lit. *They were mentioned in a match.*

They were engaged through matchmaking.

Matchmaking was common in Ireland until the middle of the last century but did not always work for everybody. For many families the *spré* (dowry) was more important than love. Sometimes a young woman might have to marry an old man if he was well off and if that's what her parents wanted. Very often the woman had no say in the matter. Some of our great writers capture this predicament brilliantly. One of Liam Ó Flaithearta's characters says, '*Tá mé díolta acu mar a bheadh banbh muice*' ('They have sold me like a piglet'). Máirtín Ó Cadhain describes it thus: *Phós Micil an céad punt, na cúpla bearach agus Bríd* (Micil married the hundred pounds, the few heifers and Bríd).

The Gift of the Gab

Chuirfeadh sé caint síos i mbuidéal.

Lit. *He would put talk down into a bottle.*

He never shuts up. He is a compulsive talker.

Bhí an iomarca faid ar a theanga.

Lit. *His tongue was too long.*

He said too much.

Caint san aer.

Lit. *Talk in the air.*

Useless talk and making false promises.

Comhrá cois cabhantair.

Lit. *A conversation that takes place beside a counter.*

Pub talk. Normally, but not always, takes place beside the counter or on the high stool in a bar and not to be taken seriously. Where people are well oiled and talk (rubbish) about their big plans, which will mostly be forgotten about the next day. There is a proverb in Irish which says, *Nuair a bhíonn an t-ól istigh bíonn an chiall amuigh* (When the drink is in, the sense is out).

Níor chuir sé fiacail ann.

Lit. *He did not put a tooth in it.*

He did not mince his words. He said it straight out.

Craiceann a chur ar scéal.

Lit. *To put skin or hide on a story.*

To make a story better, more plausible or polished; to embellish it.

Ní raibh sé ar chúl an chlaí.

Lit. *He was not behind the wall.*

He was blunt. Calling a spade a spade.

I gcead don chomhluadar.

Lit. *With permission from the (present) company/*
With respect to the company.

This phrase is often used by a speaker as a little
warning to his audience just as he is about to say
something lewd or vulgar, or something that might
offend some people in the audience. For example on
the day I'm writing this I've just heard a professor
of history use it in a public talk just before he said,
'*Níorbh fhiú cac circe é*' (He wasn't worth a hen's shit).

Tharraing sé anuas an scéal.

Lit. *He pulled down the story.*

He brought up the subject.

Bhí go maith is ní raibh go holc.

Lit. *It was good and it was not bad.*

Things were good and things weren't bad/
Life was good and life wasn't bad.

This phrase has no real meaning but has been used
by storytellers for centuries when telling stories. It
might be inserted several times in the same story.
One reason would perhaps have been to give the
storyteller a chance to draw breath and think about
the next part of the story. Or it may have been said
to give the listeners some time to let the story sink
in. Sometimes it might take the storyteller two or
three nights to tell a complete story. While the
phrase is still used by storytellers today, it is also
used by people in general when telling a tale or
describing an event. It might also be translated as
'meanwhile' or 'that was all well and good'.

I ndeireadh na dála.

Lit. *At the end of the gathering.*

When all is said and done.

Anois, céard a déarfá le Gaillimh. (*And sometimes added*) Is gan ann ach baile beag.

Lit. *Now, what would you say to Galway?*
And it's only a small town.

A phrase indicating surprise. It has no meaning but is like an exclamation mark. Said when someone has unexpectedly achieved something great, having been an underdog in a situation.

Má thuigeann tú leat mé.

Lit. *If you understand me with you.*

If you understand.

Fuair sé gaoth an fhocail.

Lit. *He got wind of the word.*

He got a hint.

Ola ar a chroí.

Lit. *Oil on his heart.*

Music to his ears.

Dúirt bean liom gur dhúirt bean léi.

Lit. *A woman told me that a woman told her.*

Hearsay. One of the few Irish language phrases
that is also used in everyday spoken English in
Ireland. There is also a longer version of this phrase
sometimes used: *Dúirt bean liom gur dhúirt bean léi gur dhúirt
bean eile* … (A woman told me that a woman told her
that another woman …).

Scéal scéil.

Lit. *A story's story.*

Hearsay.

Scéal/caint i mbarr bata.

Lit. *Story/talk on top of a stick or baton.*

Senseless talk, not to be believed.

Rinne sé paidir chapaill de.

Lit. *He made a horse's prayer out of it.*

Said when someone is telling a story and drags it on and on. Another version of it would be *Scéal an Ghamhna Bhuí* (The tale of the yellow calf/yearling).

Bad Behaviour

Íde na muc is na madraí.

Lit. *The abuse of the pigs and the dogs.*

To abuse someone badly.

Thug siad íde na muc is na madraí don fhear bocht (They gave pigs' or dogs' abuse to the poor man).

Thug sé cúpla snaidhm maith dó.

Lit. *He gave him a few good knots.*

He gave him a few strong blows.

Hitting someone with a knotted rope would be a lot more painful than with a plain rope. Perhaps the phrase comes from the time when faction fights were common.

Íde béil.

Lit. Abuse of the mouth.

To give out to a person.

Thug sé íde béil dom (He gave out to me), or *Ba mhaith uaidh íde béil a thabhairt* (He was good at giving out).

Tá sé (suas) go muinéal ann.

Lit. He is (up) to his neck in it.

To be heavily involved in something,
normally something bad.

Bhuail sé isteach é ar an 'in ainm an Athar'.

Lit. He hit him on 'in the name of the Father'.

He hit him on the forehead.

When you're blessing yourself you put your right
hand to your forehead and say, '*In ainm an Athar*'
('In the name of the Father').

Gabh i leith amach ar an tsráid.

Lit. *Come over here out on the street.*

An invitation to fight in a fair way, probably with just bare fists and kicks. This phrase would normally be said in a public bar and the reason to go outside would be so as not to cause any damage inside and to have plenty of room. Another way of saying it is *Gabh i leith amach ar an bhfair play* (Come out here where there is fair play). *Chaith sé de a sheaicéad* (He threw off his jacket) is also said when preparing for a fight.

Speirfidh mé tú.

Lit. *I will cripple you.*

To inflict irreversible physical damage on someone. Comes from *ainmhí a speireadh* (to hough or hock an animal), that is to damage the joint between the knee and the fetlock in the hind leg. This was sometimes done by the Whiteboys to a landlord's cattle as an act of revenge.

Bhí an lasair sa bharrach.

Lit. *The flame was in the flax.*

To let all hell break loose. To start a row.
To inflame passions.

Often used in a sports commentary when a team
really gets going.

Bhí an nimh san fheoil acu dá chéile.

Lit. *They had poison in the flesh for each other.*

Intending to kill someone.

One way to do this was to put poison in meat or
drink, especially if the killer had no other weapon
or was not physically strong.

Ag brú gaoil air.

Lit. *Pushing kin or friendship on him.*

Trying to be close to someone (perhaps, although
not necessarily, a distant relative or acquaintance)
but with an ulterior motive.

Capall do chomharsan is do mhaide féin.

Lit. *Your neighbour's horse and your own stick.*

Taking advantage of a neighbour's generosity.

Not all families could afford a horse or donkey and would borrow an animal from a neighbour for a day or two to do some work. Some people might, however, try to work a neighbour's animal twice as hard as its owner would.

Ní raibh ann ach troid na mba maol.

Lit. *It was only the fight between hornless cows.*

A harmless fight, normally between friends.

The word *maol* in Irish means bald, but when applied to a cow it means hornless. When hornless cows fight they don't really hurt each other. The phrase is often used nowadays to describe the antics of politicians and the like.

Thit sé ina scraith/Rinneadh scraith de.

Lit. *He fell in a scraw/He was made into a scraw.*

He was floored.

Very often used by sports commentators when commentating on boxing or GAA matches, but also used if someone is floored in a pub brawl.

Bhí an chloch sa mhuinchille aige dó.

Lit. *He had the stone in the sleeve for him.*

Being out to get someone, to settle a score.

Likely to originate from the time people used stones to fight, which they could hide up their sleeve until they would be near their target.

Thug mé na cosa liom.

Lit. *I took the legs with me.*

I got away with it.

Perhaps this phrase comes from a time when a person had to run for his life from animals or another person in order to be safe or survive.

Feicfidh mé arís tú.

Lit. *I will see you again.*
I will pay my bill later.

Not a welcome phrase and normally associated with a person who doesn't like to put his hand in his pocket to pay for something he owes. A mean person could be described thus: *Ní raibh aige ach feicfidh mé arís tú* (All he had was I will see you again).

Getting Down to Business

Obair na gcapall.

Lit. *The work of horses.*

Hard work.

Bhain sé deatach as.

Lit. *He got smoke out of it.*

To take a lot out of an animal or a person.

To work or play hard.

Bhain sé deatach as an gcapall (He rode the horse hard).

Na caoirigh / ba a chur thar abhainn.

Lit. *To put the sheep/cattle over the river.*

To get the job done.

Ní bhuailfeadh sé tóin bó le sluasaid.

Lit. *He wouldn't hit a cow's arse with a shovel.*

Said a about a person who would be useless at work,
sport or in general.

Is ait an fear é lá fliuch.

Lit. *He's a mighty man on a wet day.*

Said about a person who is all talk and no action,
implying that he is useless at working.

Bhí sé ag dul ó phosta go piléar.

Lit. *He was going from post to pillar.*

He was getting nowhere/accomplishing nothing.

Ag gabháil dá thóin in airde.

Lit. *Going around with his arse in the air.*

Said about a person who should be doing something, but is actually doing nothing.

Ní raibh an dara suí sa bhuaile aige.

Lit. *He did not have the second sitting in the booley.*

He worked very hard because he had to.

From the word *buaile* we have the English word booley. The booley was a milking place or a small pen or enclosure for sheep or cows, a place to shelter. It is in several Irish place names, for example *An Bhuaile*/Booley in Co. Wexford.

Cic sa tóin páighe an asail.

Lit. *A kick in the arse is the donkey's wages.*

Said when a person's work is not appreciated.

Lá na coise tinne.

Lit. *The day of the sore foot.*

The day you couldn't work.

Chuir sé an pionna ionam.

Lit. *He put the pin or peg in me.*

He fooled me. Normally said when a person makes a
bad business deal.

Ordóga uilig é.

Lit. *He is all thumbs.*

He is not good with his hands.

Fuair sé an craiceann is a luach.

Lit. *He got the hide and its value.*

He got double the price.

This comes from a famous folk tale, *An Craiceann is a Luach*, where the mother sends her son out to the market with a sheep's hide and tells him not to come home without the value of the hide and the hide itself. He comes home the first two days with just the hide as no one would buy it from him because he would not let the buyer have the hide. On the third day someone advises him to sell the wool on the hide, which he does and then returns home with the hide and its value.

The opposite, *Ní bhfuair sé an craiceann ná a luach* (He got neither the hide nor its value), is also a very common phrase. It means he was left with little or nothing.

Cothrom na Féinne.

Lit. *The fairness of the Fianna.*

Fair play.

The Fianna were famous for *glaine ár gcroí, neart ár ngéag, agus beart de réir ár mbriathar* (our clear conscience, the strength of our limbs and honouring our word). This can be used in all walks of life.

Cothrom na Féinne na haimsire.

Lit. *The fair play of the weather.*

To get enough good weather to do the work.

I only ever heard this phrase once, from an elderly man in Indreabhán. As I was walking the bog road he was saving turf, which takes about four weeks of good weather to dry. It was a bad, wet summer but he had not lost hope and said to me, '*Is beag bliain nach bhfaigheann muid Cothrom na Féinne na haimsire*' ('It's a rare year we don't get a fair share of good weather to do the work or save the harvest').

Muc i mála.

Lit. *A pig in a poke.*

Something you wouldn't buy or accept without checking beforehand.

This is a very common phrase, which can be used in any situation, even to describe a political agreement. *Fuair sé muc i mála* (He got a pig in a poke) would be a bad deal. Poke is an informal word for a bag. Piglets would normally be transported by farmers to the markets and fairs in bags, and while the potential buyer might hear the squeals, it would be highly recommended to him not to buy without opening the bag first and checking he wasn't inadvertently buying a bag of cats!

Thug sé bata agus bóthar dom.

Lit. *He gave me the stick/baton and the road.*

He dismissed me.

É a chur ar an leabhar.

Lit. *To put it on the book.*

To put it on the slate. To hold off payment until a later date.

Until the middle of last century in many shops in rural Ireland there was a book of accounts listing what each family or customer owed. The bill would often be settled with money from America or emigrants, commonly around Christmas time.

Ualach ghiolla na leisce.

Lit. *The load of the lazy servant.*

This is said about a person who tries to carry everything in one big load (and drops everything) instead of two smaller loads.

Bhí sé le fáil ar ardú orm/ar amhrán.

Lit. It was to be got by lifting it onto my back/for a song.

To get something for little or nothing.

Singers might not agree! Just as you have buskers and street singers nowadays, it was once common to have singers and musicians at fairs and pattern days, singing and playing music for whatever coins or little money people could offer them. The English phrase 'singing for your supper' would likely come from this sort of situation also.

Human Emotion

Tá an cac curtha suas ann.

Lit. *The shit is shoved up in him.*

Chroith sé an cac ann/as.

Lit. *He shook the shit in him/out of him.*

Chuir sé an builín suas ann.

Lit. *He put the loaf up in him.*

Ar crith ina chraiceann.

Lit. *Shaking in his skin.*

All these are ways of saying someone is afraid.

Bhí sé le ceangal.

Lit. *He needed to be tied.*

He was fit to be tied, i.e. he was very angry or mad.

In older times if someone was drunk from drinking poitín and out of his mind, the custom was to tie him up with a rope until he came to his senses so that he would not harm himself or other people. My fellow Connemara writer Pádraic Breathnach remembers such an incident from his childhood days in Moycullen in the 1950s: 'I remember my father coming home from a wedding celebration in Aubwee to fetch a rope to tie a relative of his who had been fighting because he had too much poteen to drink. The wedding was being celebrated in the couple's new house and not a window was left unbroken.'

Chuir sé an croí/cac trasna ionam.

Lit. *He put the heart/shit across in me.*

He scared me to death.

Bhí sé ag cur a chraicinn de.

Lit. *He was shedding his skin.*

He was raging mad, giving out.

This could also describe a singer who was singing his head off, or a person who was very excited about something.

Bhí a thóin amuigh.

Lit. *His arse was out.*

He was put out, or sulking.

Dá mbeadh breith ar m'aiféala agam.

Lit. *If I could catch my regret.*

If I could change the past. If I got a second chance.

In umar na haimléise.

Lit. *In the font of misery or wretchedness.*

To be in a miserable state. In a fix.
Down in the dumps.

Tá an oiread gráin aige air is atá ag an diabhal ar uisce coisreacain.

Lit. *He hates it as much as the devil hates holy water.*

To really despise something.

Ní raibh cíos, cás ná cathú orm.

Lit. *I didn't have rent, concern or temptation
(to bother me).*

I was carefree. I hadn't a care in the world.

Chuir sé crith magairlí orm.

Lit. *He made my testicles shake.*

Quaking with fear.

Tá sé imithe le craobhacha.

Lit. *He has taken to the branches.*

He has gone mad.

This refers to *Buile Shuibhne* (The Frenzy or Madness of Sweeney), a twelfth-century tale. Suibhne Mac Colmáin was a king in Ulster. St Rónán put a curse on him and he was banished to wander Ireland, completely insane. Some versions of the legend say he took to the air and flew all over the country, sleeping in trees at night and in glens, one of them being *Gleann na nGealt* (Glannagalt) on the Dingle peninsula in Co. Kerry. It means the 'glen of the mad/lunatics'. It was believed that a cure for insanity existed in a well there. There are many stories of raving mad people going to *Gleann na nGealt* and leaving it cured.

Bhí a theanga bheag amuigh le dúil ann.

Lit. He had his little tongue out desiring it.

When a person wants something badly.

This would normally apply to drink, food or sex. In Irish *teanga bheag* (small tongue) describes the uvula. Another term for the uvula is *sine scórnaí* (literally, throat nipple).

Scéal fada ar an anró.

Lit. A long story about the hardship.

Normally said about a person who is always complaining or feeling sorry for himself.

Comparisons

Like most other languages there are hundreds of comparisons in Irish. You will find the typical ones you find in other languages such as: *chomh crua le cloch* (as hard as a rock), *chomh geal le sneachta* (as white as snow), *chomh fuar leis an mbás* (as cold as death), but here is a small collection of the most colourful ones.

Chomh fada siar is atá an bia sa bhfaocha.

Lit. *As far back as the food is in the periwinkle.*

Periwinkles were a common diet for people along the coast. They would be boiled and then the food would be picked out of the shell with a needle, which could be difficult at times as the winkle might have crouched back in the shell.

Chomh buí le cos lachan.

Lit. *As yellow as a duck's leg.*

A lyrical way of saying something is yellow.

Chomh dubh le hanam tincéara.

Lit. *As black as a tinker's soul.*

A slur of course and not recommended for use, but I have included it here as it reflects an important part of our social history. In most of the schoolbooks I read as a child, Travellers would nearly always be portrayed as dishonest people, stealing chickens, etc., from the settled community. This phrase reveals the deep-seated prejudice against Travellers among the Irish settled community. Nowadays of course, we are more reflective about this injustice, but the language still contains the slur.

Chomh caoch le gandal.

Lit. As blind as a gander.

The English equivalent of this would be
'as blind as a bat'.

Chomh lag le héinín gé.

Lit. As weak as a gosling.

Unlike some other small birds, if the gosling
tumbles and find itself lying on its back it can't get
up again without help.

Chomh gaisciúil/postúil le cat siopa.

Lit. As boastful as a shop cat.

The shopkeeper's cat would normally have plenty
and would be well fed with bits and pieces of meat
and all sorts of leftovers as compared to ordinary
village cats.

Chomh lite le lao óg.

Lit. *As licked as a young calf.*

Said about a person who is well groomed.

Chomh scaipthe le bricfeasta madra.

Lit. *As scattered as a dog's breakfast.*

A dog's breakfast would often be bits and pieces of
leftovers thrown to him at intervals when people
finished eating.

Chomh bog/mín le tóin páiste.

Lit. *As soft/smooth as a baby's bum.*

Chomh fada le ráithe an earraigh.

Lit. *As long as the season of spring.*

Chomh sean leis na ciaróga/leis an gceo.

Lit. *As old as the beetles/as the fog.*

Chomh cam le corrán/
Chomh cam le hadharc reithe.

Lit. *As crooked as a sickle/As crooked as a ram's horn.*

Chomh díomhaoin le laidhricín píobaire.

Lit. *As idle as a piper's little finger.*

The piper does not use one of his little fingers
(depending on whether he is left-handed or right-
handed) when playing the uilleann pipes.

Chomh cinnte is atá tú beo.

Lit. *As sure as you're alive.*

This would be used to emphasise something,
to really push a point home.

64

Chomh cinnte is atá cac san asal.

Lit. *As sure as there is shit in the donkey.*

As sure as can be, as sure as you are standing there.

Chomh luaineach leis an ghaoth Mhárta.

Lit. *As changeable/as fickle as the March wind.*

Chomh sleamhain le heascann.

Lit. *As slippery as an eel.*

Hard Times

Caite i dtraipisí.

Lit. *Thrown with the discarded articles.*

Thrown away. Consigned to the scrap heap.
Forgotten about.

Tá sé caite sna fataí lofa.

Lit. *He was thrown in the rotten potatoes.*

He was discarded.

This could be used in many situations, such as a
person being left off a football team, being sacked
from their job, or thrown out of a nightclub.

Bhí sé i ladhar an chasúir aige.

Lit. *He had him in the claw of a hammer.*

To be between a rock and a hard place.

Bhí mé idir dhá thine Bhealtaine.

Lit. *I was between two May (day) fires.*

To be in a dilemma.

This refers to the traditional practice of driving cows between two bonfires, which would be lit for this purpose on *Lá Bealtaine* (1 May, May Day). It was considered a purification ritual. May Day, the beginning of summer, was a very important date in the Celtic calendar as was *Lá Samhna* (1 November), the beginning of winter. Important festivals (*féilte*) were held: *Féile na Bealtaine* and *Féile na Samhna*. Hence the phrase *Ó Shamhain go Bealtaine* (from November to May).

An chloch is mó ar mo phaidrín.

Lit. *The biggest stone/bead on my rosary.*

My biggest worry. The most important item
on my agenda.

The phrase is likely to come from the fact that some
rosaries have bigger beads between each section
(decade) to remind the person who is saying the
rosary that one decade is ending and another
beginning.

Níl aige ach ón láimh go dtí an béal.

Lit. *All he has is from the hand to the mouth.*

He is poor, living from hand to mouth.

Snámh in aghaidh an easa.

Lit. *To swim against the waterfall.*

To strive against the odds.
Trying to do the impossible.

An bád bán (Thug sé an bád bán air féin).

Lit. *The white boat (He took the white boat on himself).*

He emigrated.

An bád bán refers to a white passenger ship which brought Irish emigrants abroad, to Britain or the USA. From this the phrase *Thug sé an bád bán air féin* came into the language. Most of the currachs and small boats people used when fishing or working were black, but the big white boat was a symbol of emigration. And while very few people emigrate by boat nowadays, the phrase is still very much in use to describe emigration.

Ar an trá fholamh.

Lit. *On the empty strand.*

To be left with nothing, empty-handed.

The strand and the sea were important sources of fish and food, especially during famine times.

Féar dhá ghabhar agus sean-asal.

Lit. *The grass of two goats and an old donkey.*

Used to describe someone who was poor.

In older times wealth was measured not by money but by land and farm animals. *Féar dhá bhó agus capall* (The grass of two cows and a horse), while not much above the poverty threshold, would be a big step up from the grass of two goats and an old donkey. A family could survive and have just about enough to eat on a farm that could support a couple of cows and a horse.

Sin í an iarraidh a mharaigh an mhuc.

Lit. *That was the blow that killed the pig.*

The English equivalent is 'The straw that broke the camel's back'. Instead of camels, there were plenty of pigs in Ireland. Most small farmers would raise one or two of them to help pay the rent.

Bhí mé i m'Oisín i ndiaidh na Féinne.

Lit. *I was like Oisín after the Fianna.*

I was left behind. Completely lost.

This is from the folktale about Oisín, when he was given permission to return from *Tír na nÓg* (the Land of Youth) and visit Ireland on strict condition he would not set foot on the land. But he fell off his horse while trying to help a few men lift a rock and when his foot touched the ground he aged 300 years. He could not return to *Tír na nÓg* and all his Fianna friends were long dead, so he was left behind knowing nobody.

Cuid Pháidín den mheacan.

Lit. *Paudeen's share of the carrot.*

The useless part. The long, thin tail-end of the carrot that is cut off and thrown away.

Usually used to describe a person who gets a bad deal or only the leftovers.

Áit na leathphingine.

Lit. *The halfpenny's place.*

A cheap or unimportant place.

Often used to describe a person who is left high and dry or who got a bad deal. This concept was made famous by the opening lines of Máirtín Ó Cadhain's classic novel *Cré na Cille*, where corpses are buried in certain parts of the graveyard according to their status in their previous life: *'Ní mé an ar Áit an Phuint nó na Cúig Déag atá mé curtha? D'imigh an diabhal orthu dhá mba in Áit na Leathghine a chaithfidís mé, th'éis ar chuir mé d'fhainiceachaí orthu!'* ('I wonder am I buried in the Pound Plot or the Fifteen-Shilling Plot? Or did the devil possess them to dump me in the Half-Guinea Plot, after all the warnings I gave them?').

Chuaigh sé thar loch amach.

Lit. *He went out over the lake.*

He emigrated.

The Demon Drink

D'ólfadh sé anuas as thóin muice.

Lit. *He would drink from a pig's arse.*

D'ólfadh sé anuas as thóin gadhair.

Lit. *He would drink from a dog's arse.*

D'ólfadh sé aníos as *wellington*.

Lit. *He would drink out of a wellington.*

D'ólfadh sé an chrois.

Lit. *He would drink the cross.*

These are all ways to describe a heavy drinker.

D'ólfadh sé an braon anuas.

Lit. He would drink the drop down.

This means he would drink anything, including the sooty water oozing out of the chimney-stack or through a gap in the ceiling.

Bhí braon maith sa gcoiricín aige.

Lit. He had a good drop in the crest.

He had a good drop of drink taken.

The crest is the tuft of feathers on top of a bird's head. Also used in *Dul i gcoiricín a chéile* (To go at each other's crest, to fight).

Bhí sé ar leathmhaing.

Lit. He was slanted.

He had a lot of drink taken.

Rinne sé deoch chapaill de.

Lit. *He made a horse's drink out of it.*

A strong drink, when someone pours a glass of whiskey into his pint.

Bhí sé ag tabhairt dhá thaobh an bhóthair leis.

Lit. *He was taking both sides of the road with him.*

In other words, he was walking in a zig-zag manner, unable to walk in a straight line.

D'ól sé buidéal parlaimint.

Lit. *He drank a bottle of parliament.*

Meaning he drank a bottle of alcohol on which tax was paid to the government (parliament) as compared to poitín, which would have been distilled and sold illegally and tax-free of course.

Bhí a inchinn sa leathcheann aige.

Lit. *His brain was tilted to one side of his head.*

He was drunk out of his skull.

Beidh deoch an dorais againn.

Lit. *We will have a drink for the door.*

We'll have one for the road. Last round.

Personality Traits

Níl tóin ná ceann air.

Lit. *There is no arse nor head on him.*

He is neither here nor there.
Someone who can't be figured out.

Is maith leis *jam* a bheith ar dhá thaobh an cháca aige.

Lit. *He likes to have jam on both sides of the bread.*

He wants it both ways, to have his cake and eat it.

Ní haon ribín réidh é.

Lit. *He is no easy ribbon.*

He is no pushover. He is not easy to deal with.

Tadhg an dá thaobh.

Lit. *Tadhg of the two sides.*

Two-faced. Keeping in with both sides.

Gan barr cleite isteach ná bun cleite amach.

Lit. *Not a top feather [sticking] in nor a bottom feather [sticking] out.*

This would refer to somebody who is very neat and very prim and proper.

Ó! mo chuimhne is mo dhearmad.

Lit. *Oh, my memory and my forgetfulness.*

This phrase is said when you suddenly remember you wanted to say something to someone, but had forgotten what it was.

Déirc Uí Bhriain is a dhá shúil ina dhiaidh.

Lit. *O'Brien's alms and his two eyes after it.*

When a person gives alms grudgingly, generally denoting someone who is mean.

Who the original O'Brien was, who knows? It's a very common surname in Ireland.

Dhéanfadh sé nead i do chluais.

Lit. *He would make a nest/web in your ear.*

Said about a person who is cunning, who would take advantage of you right under your nose. The word *nead* in Irish, as well as being the word for a bird's nest, is the word for web, as in a spider's web: *nead damháin alla*.

Díolfadh sé agus cheannódh sé arís thú.

Lit. *He would sell you and buy you again.*

He would fool you. Pull the wool over your eyes.

Chuirfeadh sé an dubh ina gheal ort.

Lit. *He would convince you that black is white.*

Refers to somebody who is very clever and very
persuasive.

Tuigeann Tadhg Taidhgín.

Lit. *Tadhg understands Taidhgín.*

A nod is as good as a wink.

There is also a proverb in Irish: *Is leor nod don eolach*
(A nod is enough for those in the know).

Being Human

Chonaic sé an dá shaol.

Lit. *He saw both lives.*

He lived through the good and the bad times.

Tá saol an mhadra bháin aige.

Lit. *He has the life of the white dog.*

He has a great, easy life, the life of Reilly.

Perhaps at some time a breed of white dogs that were pets, not working dogs like sheep dogs, was introduced into the countryside by the gentry.

Tá sé imithe sna cearca fraoigh.

Lit. *He has gone and joined the grouse hens.*

He's for the birds. He's gone off in a tangent.

Said about someone who would make a drastic (often sudden) change in his lifestyle.

Táim ag baint lá as.

Lit. *I'm taking a day out of it [life].*

Living from day to day. To be just existing.

Bíonn faithní ar shúile daoine scaití.

Lit. *Sometimes people have warts in their eyes.*

Sometimes people don't see (or choose not to see) things.

Bhí sé ar leathshúil.

Lit. *He was on a half eye.*

He had only one eye.

In Irish *leath* (half) is used for one when referring to body parts or organs of which there are two. *Leathlámh* is one-handed; *leathchos*: one-legged; *leathchluas*: one-eared; *leathchíoch*: one-breasted; *leathmhagairle*: one-testicled.

When referring to drinking, *leathcheann* (half-one) or *leathghloine* (half a glass) is a measure of whiskey, not half a glass. Therefore, *pionta agus leathcheann* means a pint and a measure of whiskey, not a pint and a half!

Tá sé imithe ar an uisce bruite.

Lit. *He is gone on the boiled water.*

He has lost weight.

Tá a chosa nite.

Lit. *His feet are washed.*

Tá a phort seinnte.

Lit. *His tune is played.*

Tá a rás rite.

Lit. *His race is run.*

Tá a chnaipe déanta.

Lit. *His button is done.*

Tá a chuid fataí ite.

Lit. *His potatoes are eaten.*

All of the above are used to note that a person is dead. The reference to the feet being washed is likely to refer to the washing of the corpse after death.

Tá sé tite i bhfeoil.

Lit. *He is fallen into flesh.*

He has gained weight.

Ní raibh oiread Áiméan ann.

Lit. *There was not as much as an Amen in him.*

Used to describe someone who is very weak or feeble. It can also mean very small and could be used to describe a very small bird or animal. Perhaps it originated as a description of a dying person who would be too weak to say the word *Áiméan* in reply to prayers.

Bhí sé ina chraiceann dearg.

Lit. *He was in his red skin.*

He was naked.

Cadhan aonair.

Lit. *Lone bird.*

To be alone.

It has been said that this refers to a heron, a solitary bird. *Tá sé ina chadhan aonair ó bhásaigh a bhean* (He is all alone since his wife died).

Go pioctha bearrtha.

Lit. *Picked and shaved.*

Neat and tidy. To be spruced up.

Isteach cluas amháin agus amach cluas eile/ Thug sé an chluas bhodhar dom.

Lit. *In one ear and out the other/He gave me the deaf ear.*

He did not listen to me.

Saol fata i mbéal muice.

Lit. *The life of a potato in a pig's mouth.*

Used to describe a very short life.

Bhí a cháil bailithe roimhe.

Lit. *His fame had gone before him.*

He was famous.

Duine mór le rá.

Lit. *A person who is big to say.*

A person who is talked about a lot, or who is famous.

Aire an éin ghé.

Lit. *The care of the gosling.*

To take great care of something, or, indeed, a
person.

Tá sé i ngalar na gcás.

Lit. *He is in the disease of indecision.*

Tá sé idir dhá chomhairle.

Lit. *He is between two minds.*

Idir dhá cheann na meá.

Lit. *Between both ends of the weighing scale.*

All three of these mean being in two minds, trying
to make your mind up.

Tá an saol ar a thoil aige.

Lit. *He has life the way he wills it.*

He has a good or easy life.

A leath deridh.

Lit. *His end half.*

His arse, rear end.

Daily Life

Tá sé imithe amach chuig teach an asail.

Lit. *He is gone out to the donkey's house.*

He is gone out to the toilet.

Until the middle of last century most houses did not
have indoor toilets or bathrooms, so people would
have to go outside to relieve themselves. On a rainy
day they would more than likely use the cowshed or
the donkey's hut.

Ní ligfeadh sé luch as pholl ná diabhal as ifreann.

Lit. *It wouldn't let a mouse out of a hole nor
the devil out of hell.*

Used to describe a very rainy day.
The sort of a day you wouldn't put the dog out.

Chuaigh sé amach ag scaoileadh cnaipe.

Lit. *He went out to undo a button.*

He went out for a shit.

In my younger days most men and boys wore braces instead of belts. The simple way to go to the toilet, especially if you wore a jumper or jacket, would be to go down on your hunkers and undo the buttons at the back of the braces.

Samhradh beag na ngéanna.

Lit. *The small summer of the geese.*

An Indian summer.

Bhí sé ina chaitheamh sceana gréasaí.

Lit. *It was throwing cobblers' knives.*

Heavy rain. It was raining cats and dogs.

A cobbler's knife would be very sharp to cut leather.

Lá faoin gclaí.

Lit. *A day in the wall.*

A rainy day. Not much work could be done and people would shelter behind a stone wall.

Tá sé in am soip.

Lit. *It's time for the stub or straw.*

It is time to go to bed.

Before mattresses were common, or before many people could afford them, people used to sleep on straw beds or beds made from rushes. *In am soip* can also mean it's time for a nightcap.

Codladh an tsicín ort.

Lit. *The chicken's sleep on you.*

Protracted sleep. A long sleep.

Tá sé imithe sa bhfraoch orm.

Lit. *It's gone into the heather on me.*

To lose or mislay something.

A small thing lost or dropped in the heather would
be hard to find.

Chroch sé a chuid seolta.

Lit. *He raised his sails.*

He went off.

I ndeireadh na bliana a rugadh tú.

Lit. *At the end of the year you were born.*

Said to a person who is late, for example if someone
is late for dinner. The opposite is also said to
someone who is early: *I dtús na bliana a rugadh tú* (At the
beginning of the year you were born).

Bhuail sé ráille.

Lit. *He hit the rail.*

He left.

D'íosfadh sé cloch fhaobhair.

Lit. *He would eat a whetstone.*

A whetstone is a sharpening stone used to sharpen
knives and other cutting tools.

D'íosfadh sé gan salann é.

Lit. *He would eat him/it without salt.*

Very hungry.

Age

Is iomaí craiceann a chuireann an duine de.

Lit. *It's many a skin a person sheds.*

To go through many phases or ages.

Mostly said about a young person when he makes a mistake or does not yet have the same understanding of life as an older person would have.

Tá na cúlfhiacla curtha go maith aige.

Lit. *His back [wisdom] teeth are well sown/grown.*

He is grown up. He is no spring chicken.

Normally said about an animal, but could be said about a person too.

Aois na Caillí Béarra.

Lit. *The age of the Hag of Beara.*

Very old.

An Chailleach Bhéarra (the Hag of Beara) is one of the oldest mythological beings associated with Ireland according to legend. She is particularly associated with the Beara peninsula in west Cork. She is said to have had seven periods of youth, one after the other, so that every man who lived with her died of old age before her. Patrick Pearse begins his famous poem 'Mise Éire' with a reference to her: *Mise Éire, sine mé ná an Chailleach Bhéarra* (I am Ireland, older than the Hag of Beara).

Bhí siad ansin sular rugadh Dia.

Lit. *They were there before God was born.*

They're as old as the hills.

Tá siad ansin ó bhí an diabhal ina pháiste.

Lit. *They're there since the devil was a child.*

They've been there for ages.

Le haois gadhair.

Lit. *For a dog's age.*

For ages. For donkey's years.

Ag déanamh a anama.

Lit. *Making his soul.*

Repenting, getting ready for the next life.

This was normally said about old people: *Tá sé in am aige siúd a bheith ag déanamh a anama* (It's time for him to be getting ready to meet his maker). You would often hear this phrase said about an old person who was going out gallivanting or staying out late where there was music and song.

Tá sé ag titim siar ar a chuid maidí.

Lit. *He is falling back on his oars.*

He is beginning to lose his power or his strength.
Giving up. Not being as good as he was once.

Tá sé ag ligean uisce isteach.

Lit. *He is letting water in.*

He is not as good as he was, he is getting old,
as in a boat that has started leaking.

Troublesome Times

Ar chraiceann do chluaise.

Lit. *By the skin of your ear.*

A warning: for your own sake.

Tá sé san fhaopach.

Lit. *He is in dire straits/in a fix.*

He is in an awkward predicament. He is stuck,
in trouble.

Tá a chac anois aige.

Lit. *Now he has his shit.*

Now he is in the shit. He's in a fix.

Tá an tóin tite as.

Lit. *The arse has fallen out of it.*

He/it has fallen apart/failed.

Bhí an phraiseach ar fud na mias.

Lit. *The mess was all over the basin.*

The shit hit the fan.

Chac sé ar na huibheacha.

Lit. *He shat on the eggs.*

He made a mess of things.

Possibly comes from a time when people used
the outhouse or henhouse as a bathroom.

Thug sé liopa mhaith den teanga dó.

Lit. *He gave him a good lip of the tongue.*

He scolded him.

Tháinig siad salach ar a chéile.

Lit. *They came dirty on each other.*

They crossed each other or hindered each other.

The phrase is often used about currach racing, when the leading currach pulls across in front of another currach to deliberately stop them from overtaking.

Ná tarraing ort é.

Lit. *Don't draw him on you.*

Don't give him the opportunity to give out to you or attack you.

Bhí sé ina ghearradh fiacal.

Lit. *Teeth were being cut.*

Arguing. Anger.

For example: *Bhí sé ina ghearradh fiacal ar an taobhlíne* (Heated arguments were being exchanged on the sideline).

Thug sé do na bonnacha é.

Lit. *He gave it to the feet.*

He ran.

D'imigh sé de rite reaite.

Lit. *He went at a run.*

He hightailed it as fast as he could.

Sa bhearna bhaoil.

Lit. *In the dangerous gap.*

Being in danger.

The word *bearna* can mean gap, mostly associated with gaps in walls. There are several place names in Ireland which use this word. *Bearna* (Barna), for example, is a small village about five miles west of Galway city. *Bearna* can also mean a pass or a way through. For armies, passing through such places could be dangerous and some are recorded in the Irish annals as the sites of military encounters. For example, in 1599 English forces led by the Earl of Essex were attacked and routed in such a place in Co. Laois by Uaithne Ó Mordha (Owny O'More) and up to 500 of Essex's soldiers were killed in the ambush. It was henceforth known as *Bearna na gCleití* (Pass of the Plumes) after all the feathers which were left on the battlefield from the helmets of the English soldiers.

Rinne sé brochán de.

Lit. *He made porridge of it.*

He made a mess of it.

Greim an fhir bháite.

Lit. *The drowning man's grip.*

To hold very tight, hold on for dear life.

Chuaigh sé go snaidhm an rópa.

Lit. *He went as far as the knot on the rope.*

He went right down to the wire. To the very end.
A close call.

More than likely related to hanging, a common way
of execution in Ireland in olden days. Also, if a rope
is being pulled from you, a knot on it could be your
last chance to grip it and your only hope to hold on
or lose all.

Is féidir leat fuarú sa gcraiceann ar théigh tú ann.

Lit. *You can cool down in the skin you heated up in.*

A way of telling someone to cool down after a heated argument.

Tháinig sé abhaile is a dhá lámh chomh fada lena chéile.

Lit. *He came home with his two hands as long as each other.*

He came home empty-handed.

When you have something and carry it under your arm, the other hand looks longer.

Go bun an angair.

Lit. *To the bottom of the distress/affliction.*

To the bitter end. To get to the bottom of the problem.

Ar mo chrann a thit sé.

Lit. *It was on my tree it fell.*

It became my responsibility, with the connotation of drawing the short straw.

From the word *crann* (tree) we get the word *crannchur* as in *An Crannchur Náisiúnta*/The National Lottery. In Irish *é a chur ar chrainn* is to draw lots where small or short twigs would often be used instead of straws.

Words of Encouragement

Beidh lá eile ag an bPaorach.

Lit. (Mr) Power will have another day.

Your day will come. You will have another day.

Very common in sporting situations — normally said as encouragement to a losing team or competitor. 'Captain' Power was a famous eighteenth-century highwayman who was active in the Waterford area. On one occasion he escaped his pursuers, taunting them with *Beidh lá eile ag an bPaorach*, which means something like 'I'll live to fight another day'. Power is still a common surname in Waterford. There are early Irish records of the name written as *Le Poer* and it was believed to be a nickname of someone who has taken a vow of poverty.

Fionnadh ort/ Fionnadh ort is ná raibh sé suaimhneach ort.

Lit. *Body hair on you/Body hair on you and may it not be peaceful on you/may it be ruffled.*

These phrases are often said by members of the audience to *sean-nós* singers when they are singing a song. They are phrases of encouragement, to urge the singer on. They are normally said between (not during) verses, so they do not disturb the concentration of the singer. There are lots more of them, such as:

Up scraitheachaí! *Up sods!*
Up Seanadh Mhach! *Seanadh Mhach is a boggy place in Connemara.*
Mustais *frog* ort! *A frog's moustache on you!*
Croch suas é! *Lift it up!*
Scaoil amach é! *Let it out!*
Scaoil amach an pocaide! *Let the billy-goat out!*
Scaoil amach an bobailín! *Let the bubble out! Let it rip!*
Mo ghoirm thú! *My applause for you!*

Má thiteann tú, ná fan le n-éirí.

Lit. *If you fall, don't wait to get up.*

Hurry on. Run.

Usually said to a child when being sent on an errand.

Thug sé cead coise (cead a chos) dó.

Lit. *He allowed him to walk or follow his feet.*

Thug sé cead a chinn dó.

Lit. *He allowed him to follow his head.*

He allowed him to go/to do as he wished.

An sméar mhullaigh.

Lit. *The top berry.*

The best. The pick of the bunch.

An té is géire scian feannadh sé.

Lit. *He with the sharpest knife let him skin (an animal or a person).*

Let the best man win the fight or argument.

Bhain sé an barr de.

Lit. *He took the top off him/it.*

He surpassed him. He was better than him.

Ní fál go haer é.

Lit. *It's not a wall to the sky/the top of the air.*

It's not impossible.

Time Together
and Time to Relax

Bhí an domhan is a mháthair ann.

Lit. *The world and its mother were there.*

Bhí tír is talamh ann.

Lit. *Land and sea were there.*

Bhí uasal agus íseal ann.

Lit. *Upper class and lower class were there.*

Several ways of saying everybody was there,
there was a great crowd.

Cá mbeidh an gabhar á róstadh anocht?

Lit. *Where will the goat be roasted tonight?*

Where will the fun or craic be tonight? Comes from
the time when people would gather together in one
place to cook an animal and it would more than
likely be a long night and a social event with singing,
music, storytelling and entertainment.

Mórsheisear.

Lit. *Big six people.*

Seven people.

This is a word that's not used very often,
mostly used by storytellers when telling stories.

Dháréag agus píobaire.

Lit. *Twelve people and a piper.*

Thirteen people. A butcher's or baker's dozen.

Bhí an áit dubh le daoine.

Lit. *The place was black with people.*

This would not be in reference to the colour of their skin but the colour of their clothes, as black was traditionally the predominant clothing colour in Gaeltacht regions.

Cath na bpunnan.

Lit. *The battle of the sheaves [of oats or wheat].*

A harmless battle or pillow fight. It originally referred to a mythical battle fought by Fionn Mac Cumhaill and his Fianna.

Snámh an duine mhairbh.

Lit. *The swim of the dead man.*

To float on one's back.

Rinne sé pollín in airde.

Lit. *He made a holeen [little hole] in the air.*

He did a somersault.

A graphic description of what happens when you do a somersault, but it was the only way we ever said it in Irish and is still very much in use. It is also used by sports commentators when someone falls head over heels.

Snámh smigín (thug sé snámh smigín dom).

Lit. *Chin swim (he gave me a chin swim).*

Swimming exercise with the head supported above water. This is the way I and most of my contemporaries living by the coast learned to swim. An older sibling would hold his or her palm under your chin and place the other hand lightly above your head so that you could splash away with your hands and legs without fear of swallowing water or going under, until you had enough confidence to swim on your own.

Snámh idir dhá uisce.

Lit. *Swimming between two waters.*

To swim beneath the surface of the water.

Níor baineadh tada as an lá amárach fós.

Lit. *Nothing was taken out of tomorrow yet.*

We have plenty of time.

Lá faoin tor/sceach.

Lit. *A day under the shrub/bush.*

A free day.

Likely originated from school mitching, when children would not go to school but instead spend a lazy day in the bushes or by the seashore until it was time to go home. The word *maidhtseáil*, which came from the English 'mitching', is used in everyday Irish nowadays: *Bhí sé ag maidhtseáil inné* (He was mitching yesterday).

Chuaigh sé ann agus a chosa beaga ag rith uaidh.

Lit. *He went there and his little feet running away from him.*

He went there in a hurry. This is not used in the sense of someone who is late and is rushing to make an appointment. It only applies to going to entertainment or fun of some sort.

Snámh ar a bholg.

Lit. *Swimming on his stomach.*

Doing the front crawl.

A Motley Crew

There are many colourful Irish phrases which don't fit easily into any category, but are worth inclusion despite this. I have gathered together some of the ones that I find most interesting in this last, general section.

Aire na huibhe.

Lit. *The care of the egg.*

Eggs were important for families to supplement their income and the women would often walk for two or three hours to a market with a basket of eggs to sell, of which they would take great care so that none would be broken. This is used in the context of something or someone highly valued and taken good care of.

Grá Dia.

Lit. *Love for God*.

A favour or good deed.

Commonly used in *Rinne sé grá Dia dom* (He did me a favour).

Lig sé a chuid maidí le sruth.

Lit. *He let his oars go with the current*.

He let his chance go.

B'fhéidir is ní móide is níl ann ach drochsheans.

Lit. *Maybe and unlikely and it's only a bad chance*.

A funny, long-winded way to say it's unlikely. Often used if one couldn't (or didn't want) to give a straight answer.

Thit sé ina chnap.

Lit. *He fell in a lump.*

Thit sé i mullach a chinn.

Lit. *He fell on the top of his head.*

Thit sé as a sheasamh.

Lit. *He fell from his standing.*

Cuireadh i ndiaidh a mhullaigh é.

Lit. *He was put after his head.*

He fell forward.

This phrase is mostly used when someone's falling is totally out of his control, if a person is tripped, or slips on something.

Cár fhág tú an óinseach?

Lit. *Where did you leave the foolish woman?*

What would you expect?

There are two words for fool in Irish depending on the gender. *Óinseach* is the appropriate word for a woman or girl and *amadán* for a man or boy. *Amadán críonna* (wise fool) is a phrase that describes a man who would not be as foolish as he would look or act and could indeed be quite wise behind it all.

Thit sé i ndiaidh a chinn.

Lit. *He fell after his head [head first].*

Thit sé i ndiaidh a chúil.

Lit. *He fell after his back.*

He fell backwards.

Bhí sé faoi bhrí na mionn.

Lit. *He was under the force or virtue of oath.*

He is sworn to tell the truth.

Bhailigh sé leis a chip is a mheanaí.

Lit. *He gathered up his lasts and his awls*
[a cobbler's tools].

This refers to somebody who is leaving and not
coming back, such as a cobbler, who might spend
some time in a village mending shoes until there
would be no more work for him to do, so he
would collect all his belongings and move on.

Ar iompú boise.

Lit. *On the turning of a palm.*

Very fast. Immediately.

Ba cheart é a chur soir.

Lit. *He should be sent east.*

He should be put into the asylum.

This originated in Connemara but is now common in all Gaeltachtaí. In Irish, *soir* means east and there was a mental asylum in Ballinasloe in east Galway where many Connemara people were sent. For a few generations in Connemara the name Ballinasloe meant only one thing: the mad house. Very often there might be little or nothing wrong with people who were sent there but, if they were signed in, it was nearly impossible to get them out. For example, people could be sent there if they disagreed with the local priest or if for some reason he did not like their attitude or way of life and forced relatives to commit them. I once heard an old woman describe a man who had returned from America and who had spent some time in an asylum there say, '*Ó, bhí sé sin i mBallinasloe Mheiricea*' ('Oh, he was in America's Ballinasloe').

The word *soir* is used in this way in these examples:
Stop, is ná cuir soir mé (Stop, and don't drive me mad);
Tá mé curtha soir aige (He has me driven mental); *Thoir a
   chríochnóidh sé* (He will end up in an asylum).
Beidh mé amuigh sa teach mhór aige (I will end up in the big
   house because of it) is a Donegal equivalent.

Níor fhiafraigh sé díom an raibh béal orm.

Lit. *He did not ask me if I had a mouth.*

He did not offer me anything to eat or drink.

Codladh gé.

Lit. *A goose's sleep.*

To be half asleep or pretending to be asleep while
being well aware of what's happening around you.

Níl sé i leabhar ná i bhfoirm.

Lit. *It's not in a book nor on a form.*

Níl sé i gclár ná i bhfoirm.

Lit. *It's not on register nor on a form.*

Níl sé i laoi ná i litir.

Lit. *It's not in a poem nor in a letter.*

These three are all used to mean it's not written down anywhere, so it has no legal standing.

Dris chosáin.

Lit. *Path briar.*

An annoying obstruction.

Nuair a tháinig an crú ar an tairne.

Lit. *When the [horse]shoe came on the nail.*

When it came to the test. When a decision had to be made. When push came to shove.

This is likely to have originated from having to put a horseshoe on a horse and shape it into place while the iron is hot.

Ag gad is gaire don scornach.

Lit. *The nearest withe/rope to the throat.*

The most important or urgent thing.

As would be the case for a person who is about to be hanged, where the phrase possibly comes from.

Sop in áit na scuaibe.

Lit. *A stub/straw instead of a brush/broom.*

A weak substitute instead of the real thing.

Mar sceach i mbéal bearna.

Lit. *Like a bush in the mouth of a gap.*

A stop-gap, weak substitute or short-term solution.

An dlaoi mhullaigh a chur air.

Lit. *To put the top/last tuft/thatch on it.*

To put the finishing touch on it; to cap it off.

The phrase came from thatching houses. *Faoi dhlaoi* means under-thatched, the last bit of work carried out when building a house.

(go) Lá Philib an Chleite.

Lit. *(to) The day of Philib with the feather.*

Never.

An Irish version of Tibb's Eve, which was an archaic way of referring to a day that didn't exist.

An dá mhar a chéile.

Lit. *The two same things or likewise.*

It's the same thing.

Bhí an fharraige ina clár.

Lit. *The sea was a board.*

Said about the sea on a very calm day.

Ceann a chur ar an bpaidrín.

Lit. *To put a head/top on the rosary.*

To start something.

Fad atá do lámh ann.

Lit. *While your hand is in it.*

While you're at it.